Making Ripples

Making Ripples

mike breaux

ZONDERVAN®

WILLOW
Willow Creek Resources

ZONDERVAN.com/
AUTHORTRACKER
follow your favorite authors

Making Ripples
Copyright © 2006 by Mike Breaux

Requests for information should be addressed to:

Zondervan, *Grand Rapids, Michigan 49530*

ISBN-10: 0-310-27253-x
ISBN-13: 978-0-310-27253-3

This edition printed on acid-free paper.

All Scripture quotations, unless otherwise indicated, are taken from the *Holy Bible: New International Version*®. NIV®. Copyright © 1973, 1978, 1984 by International Bible Society. Used by permission of Zondervan. All rights reserved.

Scripture quotations marked "LB" are taken from *The Living Bible*. Copyright © 1971 by Tyndale House Publishers, Inc., Wheaton, Illinois. All rights reserved.

Scripture quotations marked "MSG" are taken from *The Message*. Copyright © 1993, 1994, 1995, 1996, 2000, 2001, 2002. Used by permission of NavPress Publishing Group.

Scripture quotations marked "NLT" are taken from the *Holy Bible: New Living Translation*, copyright © 1996. Used by permission of Tyndale House Publishers, Inc., Wheaton, IL. All rights reserved.

Scripture quotations marked "TNIV" are taken from the *Holy Bible, Today's New International Version*™. TNIV®. Copyright © 2001, 2005 by International Bible Society. Used by permission of Zondervan. All rights reserved.

Internet addresses (websites, blogs, etc.) and telephone numbers printed in this book are offered as a resource to you. These are not intended in any way to be or imply an endorsement on the part of Zondervan, nor do we vouch for the content of these sites and numbers for the life of this book.

Photo credits are located on page 112.
Art Direction: Blum Graphic Design
Book design: Joe De Leon

Printed in the United States of America

07 08 09 10 11 12 • 21 20 19 18 17 16 15 14 13 12 11 10 9 8 7 6 5 4 3 2

To Debbie,

I'm eternally grateful.

Okay . . . I'll admit it. I've got an artsy streak. Beneath the exterior of this bald, truck-drivin', dog-lovin', broken-down old jock lies the heart of an artist. Not that I have many artistic capabilities, you understand, but art moves me. Paintings. Dance. Drama. Poetry. Architecture. Something deep inside of me responds to that kind of creativity.

Of all the art forms, music and movies touch me most. I'm awestruck by haunting melodies, creative chord structures, and tight harmonies. And I love songs that tell the kind of stories that stir your heart—the ones you just want to sing over and over again. Maybe that's why I'm a country music fan. (I know, I know—just when I was doing my best to convince you I'm artsy!) I'm a sucker for a well-crafted line and compelling dialogue, too. In fact, I don't so much watch a good movie as live it. To say I can get emotionally involved isn't the half of it.

When movies combine great writing with great photography, great acting, great directing, great sound tracks, and great story lines—well, it can literally make me cry. *A Beautiful Mind* just wrecked me. My father was a brilliant guy who wrestled with mental illness, so as the credits rolled for that movie, I sat paralyzed in the back row, sobbing like a kid really missing his dad. (And I do.)

I cried at *Hoosiers*, when Jimmy hit the game-winning shot. I lost it during *Homeward Bound*. (Dog stories tear my heart out.) Both *Schindler's List* and *Hotel Rwanda* moved my God-instilled sense of justice and made me sit and think as I wiped the tears from my face.

Believe it or not, I even cried during *Dumb and Dumber*. Cried during *Monty Python and the Holy Grail*. Cried during *Tommy Boy* and *Napoleon Dynamite*. Tears ran down my face because I couldn't stop laughing at how incredibly stupid and funny those films were.

So, what about you? What are your all-time favorite movies? *Gone with the Wind*? *Ben Hur*? *Citizen Kane*? *The Godfather*? *Finding Nemo*? *Field of Dreams*? *Crash*? *March of the Penguins*? And if you had to pick just one, what would it be?

Hard, isn't it? My mind races from *Braveheart* (I was ready to paint my face blue, put on a kilt, and fight for Scotland!) to *The Fugitive*. (I'll bet your heart was pounding, too, as Federal Marshal Girard chased Dr. Richard Kimball through that underground tunnel.) I love the quirky little flick called *The Princess Bride* and the equally goofy *What about Bob?*, starring Bill Murray as Bob Wylie, who shows up at his psychiatrist's vacation house and won't go away.

But if I had to name my all-time favorite, I'm real clear what it would be. I wouldn't be able to endorse the whole thing, but I walked out of this one thinking, "I believe that might be the most creative, well put together, clever, thought-provoking, emotionally heart-tugging, best acted movie I've ever seen in my life."

And I didn't just admire the artistry or enjoy the entertainment. I learned some very profound things—

"Life is like a box of chocolates; you never know what you're gonna get."

three of them, to be exact. The first thing I learned is, "Life is like a box of chocolates; you never know what you're gonna get." Not all moments in life are crème-filled, are they? I also learned that "Stupid is as stupid does," and that stupid has nothing to do with your IQ, but everything to do with your discernment, your decision-making ability, and your propensity for promise keeping. The third thing I learned was especially freeing for me as a speaker and communicator. I learned that I didn't have to work so hard anymore on the conclusions of my messages— from that point forward, I could just finish up with "That's all I have to say about that."

Forrest Gump is one of those movies that gripped my heart and made me think a lot about my life. Do I keep my word no matter what? Do I love the people around me in an unconditional way? Do I show respect for everyone, no matter their color, race, rank, intelligence, or ignorance? Would I be candid enough to say, "I may not be a smart man, but I know what love is?"

There's a riveting scene at the end of the movie. Forrest's wife, Jenny, who had made a lot of unwise choices in her life, dies at age thirty-five. Forrest is standing at her grave and says to her, "You died on a Saturday morning, and I had you placed here under our tree." He talks about what's going on in his life, how their son little Forrest is doing, and how much he misses her.

Then he begins to reflect on life and considers a question that really marked me. He wonders whether his momma or his friend Lieutenant Dan had it right: "Do we have a destiny, or are we all just floatin' around kinda accidental-like, like a feather on a breeze?" When I heard him say that, I thought, "That is the question everyone who ever walks this planet has to come to grips with."

A Destiny or
Accidental-Like?

When I look around our culture I see lots of people who really believe we just kind of show up accidental-like, and we just float around accidental-like, like a feather on a breeze. I used to believe it—used to float around, too. I understand how people can buy into that, because these days we're taught at a very young age that we come from nothing and we're going back to nothing. So basically everything in between is just kind of, well, nothing.

If that is true, then there is no destiny; there is no purpose. And if there is no purpose, there is no truth. If there's no truth, then there's no right, there's no wrong, and we all just kind of show up accidental-like and we float around on a breeze all the way through our lives. We make up the rules as we go.

I agree with Chuck Colson's assertion that our culture is framed by "talk-show truth." Have you ever watched any of those talk shows? Unlike music or movies, they seldom move me. Maybe that's because all these shows pretty much cover the same kind of topics. I was home with the flu one morning, surfing the channels and hoping to find *The Price Is Right* ("The Most Exciting Hour of Television"), when a talk show caught my attention. A lady was seated on the stage with five guys around her in a semicircle, and this little blue caption came up on the screen to identify her particular issue. It said this woman had had affairs with all five of her husband's brothers. I raised my eyebrows and thought, "Whoa!"

But that wasn't all. Then the host went into the audience and gave the microphone to this guy who stood up and said something like, "Hey, whatever, dude. I think if they're cool with it and he's cool with it and she's cool with it, then I say go for it!" The audience applauded and cheered. And I'm still thinking, "Whoa!"

Talk-show truth. Whatever, dude. No wonder sociologists have labeled this generation the Whatever Generation. I understand that, because if we really do just show up accidental-like—if there is no destiny, and there is no purpose, and there is no truth, and there are no rules, and there is no right or wrong—then it is all kind of a big "whatever," isn't it?

I wasn't really shocked when a recent survey of American high school students found that nearly 80 percent of them said they don't believe there's such a thing

**If there is no destiny—
then it is all kind of a big
"whatever," isn't it?**

as absolute truth. That there is no absolute right or absolute wrong. Whatever you need truth to be in the situation you're in is fine. Sixty-seven percent of those students said they regularly cheat on exams. Whatever. Sixty-six

percent said they regularly drink alcohol. Whatever. Fifty-six percent said they regularly shoplift. Whatever.

I remember when this kid came up to my daughter in high school and said, "Now, let me get this straight. Isn't it true that you Christians, like, can't have sex until you're like eighteen?" Jodi replied, "Well, actually, God's design for sex is for when you get married." He shrugged and said, "Whatever."

Take a look sometime at the website for the Bureau of Justice Statistics.* I logged on not long ago and looked up some facts about violent crime. Good news: from 1994–2003, the violent crime rate in the U.S. steadily declined. In 2005, it reached its lowest rate ever—all the way down to 5,341,410 acts of violent crime for the year! (Incidentally, 29 percent of those crimes were committed under the influence of drugs or alcohol, which tends to

---

* http://www.ojp.usdoj.gov/bjs

take "whatever" to another level.) However, although the crime rate dropped for adults, among twelve- to fifteen-year-old kids, violent crime has skyrocketed in the past twenty years—by a staggering 156 percent.

In addition to alerting us to a frightening trend, this number also demonstrates how the floating-around variety of indifference can slip into something far more callous. I heard that when a fifteen-year-old gang member was indicted for murder, his buddies were incensed that the judge would set what they considered an unrealistically high bail on their friend. They were quoted as saying in the courtroom lobby, "We don't understand what the big deal is—people die every day." Whatever.

And crime is hardly the only consequence of such a mind-set. Ever seen MTV's *Spring Break*, which documents

students' sexual excesses as they celebrate a week away from school? If you're a parent, watching that may feel a little like *Whatever—Gone Wild!*, especially when you remember that you're seeing the edited-for-television version. If you allow your kids to go unchaperoned to those popular spring break destinations, understand that you'll be putting them right in the middle of a huge "whatever," including alcohol

If we just show up accidental-like, then it's really no big deal. Right?

bingeing, sexually transmitted diseases, and all kinds of stuff. Of course, if we just kind of show up accidental-like and float around like a feather on a breeze, then it's really no big deal. Right?

Stuck

Y ou can float around accidental-like if you want to, but you cannot float around the consequences of that kind of life. That whole "sow the wind, reap the whirlwind"* deal seems pretty accurate. The truth is, there are fairly predictable outcomes to a "whatever" kind of existence. That's certainly been true in my life.

I've sometimes learned about consequences so

* Hosea 8:7

devastating to a person, it's just broken my heart. I was in Alaska to teach several years ago, and my host took me down to the Kenai Peninsula. As we drove along the Cook Inlet, I saw a huge warning sign on this incredible black beach. I asked, "What's the deal with the 'Keep Out' sign? That beach looks beautiful to me."

"Oh, that's glacial silt," he said. "You don't want to get in that stuff. It's like quicksand. You sink in that, and it wraps around you and you can't get out. So they put up those big warning signs to keep people off the beach."

Then he told me a tragic story. A honeymooning couple had rented some ATV four-wheelers and were driving all over the place, just having a blast. The woman ignored the warning signs and drove into that stuff. Then she jumped off the ATV and sank in up to her knees. At first, her husband thought it was funny, but he stopped laughing when people on the road started yelling and waving at him to stay out. Then the onlookers ran for help.

The tide was coming in, but the woman couldn't get out because this glacial silt was now up to her thighs. The fire department arrived and used pressure hoses to try to free her. But they couldn't, because the tide was even higher, more silt had accumulated, and she was stuck up to her waist.

They even brought in a helicopter to try to pull her straight out, but that effort failed as well. Despite all their heroic efforts, they were unable to save that poor woman as the tide flowed back into Cook Inlet.

Rescued by the Destiny Maker

know way too many people whose lives, spiritually and emotionally speaking, are just that stuck. They're drowning that deep and that desperate, all because they've ignored God's loving warning signs, God's boundaries, and lived life like we all just show up accidental-like and float around like a feather on a breeze. Do you know anyone in that situation? Maybe you're thinking right now,

"Yeah. Me. The truth is I feel so empty, so directionless, so desperate, so . . . stuck."

Would you allow a guy who's been where you are to let you in on some good news? There is a God who can rescue you from that stuck-ness! An incredibly loving and powerful God who can pull you out of anything, anywhere, if you're willing. He wants to give you a purpose

He's not a "whatever" kind of God. He wants to pour his love and leadership into your life.

and a destiny. He's not a "whatever" kind of God. He's the Destiny Maker, and he wants to pour his love and leadership into your life.

Look at what God has to say about you: "'For I

know the plans I have for you,' declares the LORD, 'plans to prosper you and not to harm you, plans to give you hope and a future'" (Jeremiah 29:11 TNIV). That sure doesn't sound like a "whatever" kind of existence to me! Sounds like we have a loving God who has some great plans for our lives.

Or take a look at *The Message* translation of Ephesians 1:4: "Long before he laid down earth's foundations, he had us in mind, had settled on us as the focus of his love, to be made whole and holy by his love." Out of all creation—before clouds or mountains or stars or rivers or giraffes—our Creator had us in mind. Isn't that incredibly cool? We are the "focus of his love"! Does that sound like a "whatever" kind of life to you?

Check this one out: "We are God's masterpiece. He has created us anew in Christ Jesus, so that we can do the good things he planned for us long ago" (Ephesians 2:10 NLT). You're his masterpiece! He wants to put you on display in the gallery of our world for all to see how wonderfully created you are. He has sculpted you, molded you, and uniquely shaped you to be useful in this world. He has good plans for your life.

Okay, just one more: "And I am sure that God, who began the good work within you, will continue his work until it is finally finished on that day when Christ Jesus comes back again" (Philippians 1:6 NLT). That doesn't sound like a "whatever" kind of deal, either. Sounds to me like there's a God who wants to move into our lives to do some good things in us from the inside out. And that he will keep on changing us and unfolding his plans for us until they are accomplished.

Moving from "Whatever" to "Wherever"

When I was seventeen years old, I was one of those "float around" kind of guys. Oh, I went to church, but I certainly didn't know God, and I sure wasn't interested in having him lead my life. I didn't have a clue that I could have a personal friendship with God. I just showed up at church and played the religion game. I was as insecure, selfish, and phony as a guy can get. I tried to impress my church friends as this really religious guy and my other friends as this really cool non-religious guy. I was the personification of "stupid is as stupid does"—I just didn't know it yet.

If you've ever tried to live a double life, you know how exhausting that can be. It takes an enormous amount of energy. And it gets harder and harder to lie creatively, doesn't it? The Bible says the person who takes crooked paths will be found out. Man, that is so true! When you're on a crooked path, how do you cover all your tracks? My life—and my lies about my life—started to unravel, and I sensed that there had to be a better way.

About that time, I became interested in this girl named Debbie. How can I describe her to you? Uh, "hot" might work! She was so incredibly cute and fun and real—and it was the "real" part that an exhausted phony like me found especially refreshing. I had never known anyone who genuinely loved God and lived like they really knew him. But Debbie did.

She laughed easily, never tried to impress people, and always seemed so secure with who she was. I prayed, "God, I want that in my life. And, uh . . . I'd like her, too, if that would be possible."

Our church was planning this weeklong retreat up in northern Minnesota, and some of my buddies wanted me to go. I asked them, "Is that Debbie girl going?" When they said she was, I signed up. My plan was to spend that whole week pursuing her. What I didn't realize was that God would be pursuing me as well.

That week God got hold of my heart. I have a

whole bunch of "Kodak moments" in the scrapbook of my mind—freeze-frame pictures I'll never forget. One of them is from a Friday night I sat by myself on the banks of a perfectly still, crystal-clear lake. I can remember the stars, the campfire, and the mosquitoes (the state bird of northern Minnesota!). And I remember the presence of God being so real to me. Everyone else had gone back to the cabins, and I sat alone crying. Then I did a strange thing—I raised my hands to God. This was not normal. If you did that in the church I grew up in, they would have asked, "Yes, do you have a question?"

But on that night, it was an instinctive act of surrender. There I sat, this exhausted, empty, broken teenager with his arms outstretched in an effort to finally get real with God—and to finally feel his love invade my heart.

"God, I don't want to live this way anymore," I prayed. "I want to give up. God, I'm giving you my life right now—I put it in your hands. I'm tired of living two lives. I need your forgiveness, and I want you to lead my life. And I really don't care, God—wherever you want to take me in this life, I'll go. I'm signing up tonight."

You might say that night I moved from "whatever" to "wherever." And I can't begin to tell you what a ride my life has been since I asked Jesus Christ to be my leader. Easy? No way. Trouble free? Pain free? Not a chance. But it has been a life full of adventure and passion, twists and turns, changed lives and an

Putting my life in the hands of the Destiny Maker has been an absolute blast!

ever-changing heart. Putting my life in the hands of the Destiny Maker has been an absolute blast! I've learned that he's smarter than me, wiser than me, and stronger than me. He has a great view from above, and he loves me in the most radical way.

Everyday Guidance

I've also learned that discovering God's plan for our lives is less about "finding God's will" than it is about following his voice. Often we want to know the blueprint—the details of our destiny. While God does reveal his overall plan for us through his Word, I've discovered that, if we'll listen, God also will lead us every day. He prompts us to do good things, kind things, right things, honest things, courageous things at every turn.

Have you felt those promptings? Maybe you've sensed God encouraging you to pick up the phone to call a friend who's going through a tough time, or prompting you to turn around and buy a sandwich for that homeless guy you just walked past. I've heard all manner of God's guidance resonate deep in my spirit: "Don't do that, don't go there, give this away, send her a note, stop by his office, forgive your mom." And I believe as we obey those promptings by the Holy Spirit of God, he begins to unveil his plan for our lives.

As a seventeen-year-old college freshman, following God's voice every day was a brand new experience. But I had told him "wherever," and I wanted to follow through. As I started reading the Bible more and praying more, I discovered that prayer was like this constant conversation between two people who love each other. I also found out that God really did speak to me—not in some weird "part the clouds" kind of way . . . just deep to deep.

> I discovered that prayer was like this constant conversation between two people who love each other.

One day, I left basketball practice and was riding my bike to my part-time gas station job—a route that took me by some housing projects—when here came one of those promptings: "Hey, you're early for work, why not park your bike and go play with those kids?" So I stopped and walked over to the basketball court where this little sixth grader named Willie was shooting around. I started shooting with him, and before long we had really hit it off. We enjoyed each other's company so much that I went back to see him again and again.

I learned that Willie's mom was a single parent trying to raise four kids. He didn't really have a positive male influence in his life, so I kind of adopted him as my "little brother." He'd come over to the campus and hang out with the guys, play basketball with us after practice, attend the games—even sat on the bench once (where I spent a lot of time). I continued to stop by his place as well.

After I graduated, though, I lost track of Willie. At one point, I heard he'd become a really good high school basketball player, but that was about the extent of my information. Then one day a few months ago, I answered the phone in my office to hear the question, "Is this Mike Breaux?" When I said yes, the voice continued: "The little skinny white dude with lots of hair, who played basketball?"

"Well, I'm still a white dude, but those other three things are way in the past," I answered. "Who's this?"

When I heard "This is Willie," my mind began Rolodexing through the possibilities. Willie? Did I even know a Willie? But as I hesitated, he continued: "You know, Willie from college."

Memories came flooding back as I asked, "You mean little sixth-grade, ball-playing Willie?"

"That's me," he answered.

What a trip! But when I asked what in the world Willie had been up to all these years, the conversation turned a little more serious. "Well, life has been pretty hard for me. I've struggled with some drug and alcohol addictions, even got in a little trouble. But I'm on the right track now, because I met this girl who started taking me to her church. They had a men's retreat last weekend and I went along—and I was calling you to tell you I surrendered my life to Jesus Christ while I was there."

After we'd done the verbal equivalent of high fives, he had more to tell me. "Yeah, I was in a circle with several guys and they asked how I had started my spiritual journey. I told them, 'There was this little skinny basketball player who stopped by my house and became my friend. His name was Mike Breaux and he was the first Christian I ever met.' They asked me if I meant the pastor guy at Willow Creek Church." Willie had no idea—he had lost track of me, too.

But Willie still had one more surprise to share. "Mike, I was wondering if you'd drive down here to Bloomington and baptize me."

Do you think I looked at my calendar to see if that was possible? No way! I said, "Absolutely! When?"

There are no words to describe to you the thrill it was to take Willie down into that water, bring him back up, and embrace him thirty years after I parked my bike at his playground! I would never have written "Baptize Willie" into my life master plan. His baptism was, instead, the result of two people simply following the voice of a God who wants to lead our lives in ways we've never dreamed.

Living the
Same Old Life

I think that when we fail to respond to God's promptings, we miss out on the adventure. And way too many people do just that. On the other hand, tuning in to his guidance can mean more adventure than we'd ever imagine. Most of my friends back home are shocked when they learn what I'm doing today— they can't believe how the grace of God changed that guy they knew way back when into the guy they know now. To be honest, I can hardly believe it myself. I have passion and purpose and joy surging through my veins that I never dreamed possible. God changes people!

And a lot of people are eager for change. I meet so many passionless, empty, bored people—and I can easily recognize those people because I was one. I especially notice it in guys. I watch them just doing the same stuff every day. I mean the "same old" life that just never changes. You know how it goes . . .

You get up at the same old time, shut off the same old alarm clock, walk in the same old bathroom, look at the same old face in the same old mirror, get in the same old shower, dry off with the same old towel, and put on the same old clothes.

Then you walk down to the same old kitchen, get out the same old bowl, pour the same old cereal, and eat it with the same old spoon, drink the same old coffee, read the same old paper, and kiss the same old spouse. After that you get in the same old car, drive the same old way to the same old job, sit at the same old desk, and laugh at the same old jokes the same old boss tells the same old way.

You clock out at the same old time, get back in the same old car, drive down the same old street, pull into the same old garage, hug the same old kids, walk back in the same old kitchen, and sit down and eat that same old dinner.

Finally, you walk to the same old family room, sit in the same old recliner, watch that same old *Wheel of*

Fortune, fall asleep in that same old chair, get up and go to the same old bed, ask that same old spouse that same old question, get that same old answer, then roll over and set the same old alarm clock and get up the next morning and do the same old thing all over again.

I don't want the "same old." do you? We've got one shot at this deal, so I want to live with passion.

That's the way a lot of people live. That's their life!

I don't want the "same old," do you? We've got one shot at this deal, so I want to live with passion. I want to live with a sense of purpose. I don't want to work a while, make a few bucks, build up my 401k, buy a golf cart, and spend the rest of my days trying to break par. I want to

live! Wasn't it *Braveheart*'s William Wallace who said,

"All men die. Very few ever really live"?

Making a
Difference—Now!

I heard that some researchers got a group of ninety-five-year-old men and women together and surveyed them. I don't know how they managed to do that, but they did. They asked these folks the question, "If you had it to do all over again, what would you do differently?" Can you guess what they said? Their first response may have been, "Eh, what was the question?"

But once they got it, they responded with three very specific answers.

"If we had to live life all over again," they said, "first of all, we would reflect more. We'd slow down, savor more sunsets, eat more ice cream, and laugh more. We would enjoy life more. We would soak in more special moments. We wouldn't work so fast and so feverishly."

The second thing they said was, "We'd risk more. We'd take more chances. We would live life like it's an adventure, where you can't pick the fruit unless you're out on a limb somewhere." Like an old guy said to me one day, "Son, if you ain't living on the edge, you're taking up too much space."

And third, they said, "If we had it to do all over again, we'd do something with our lives that would live on long after we're dead and gone."

I don't know about you, but I don't want to wait until I'm ninety-five to think about those things. I want

> **"If we had it to do all over again, we'd do something with our lives that would live on long after we're dead and gone."**

to reflect now. I want to risk now. I want to do something right now with my life that's going to live on long after I'm gone.

Deep down, I think all of us sense we were put on this planet to do something significant—to touch someone's life, to do some good. God, the author of goodness, put that in our DNA. Whenever I see people taking the opportunity to make a difference in another person's life, I watch them come alive! Remember, "He has created us anew in Christ Jesus, so that we can do the good things he planned for us long ago" (Ephesians 2:10 NLT). That's just an incredible way to live.

Debbie and I have two sons who are carpenters. (Yeah, that's right. I finally got that Debbie girl!) Derrick and Drew have formed a little company—Breaux Brothers Construction. We all love to build stuff, tear up stuff, and visualize what could be done with a little remodeling. The difference between them and me, though, is that they're really good at it! They're young (twenty and twenty-three), but they both have an amazing aptitude for all things construction. They also have growing hearts of compassion and a deep desire to use their skills to make a difference.

A few years back, the three of us began our own combination of *Extreme Makeover: Home Edition* and *While You Were Out* for people God put on our hearts. We try to do a project a year, because God has blessed us so much and it makes us feel alive to help out a deserving and unsuspecting family. We started by pooling our Christmas money, figuring we'd forego exchanging expensive gifts in order to watch someone else "open something." Jesus was right about that giving and receiving thing—the first option really is more fun, isn't it?

But the last project we tackled grew to a scale beyond our capabilities and resources. We had only a week to complete it, and once we got into the house, we were floored by the amount of work that had to be done. Derrick called me with the news. "This is going to take a whole lot more money and manpower than we thought. What are we going to do?"

It didn't take us long to come to two conclusions: this family really needed help, and God had asked us to provide it. If worse came to worst, I'd take out a personal equity loan to get it done. First, though, I told the guys, "Let's put out the word and see what happens."

What happened was amazing. People came out from everywhere and resources flowed like a river. We counted more than a hundred people who showed up to help that week—people who tackled projects we hadn't even planned on doing! Neighbors pitched in. Retired couples worked with us for fourteen hours a day. CEOs laid tile and painted cabinets. Teenagers landscaped. Every day, someone would swing by with lunch. One person said, "I'll buy all new appliances." A group of generous folks volunteered to buy new family room

> They saw what I've seen many
> times before—how alive
> people feel when they're a tool
> in God's hands.

furniture. Another group sprung for the counter-tops. And another for the light fixtures and vanities. A contractor re-sided the entire house for free, and when his buddy heard what we were doing, he pulled his guys off another job and had them put on a new roof in two days!

We'd just planned to renovate the kitchen, fix a few loose boards, and buy some carpet. But when all was said and done, we repaired and remodeled the entire house, made it maintenance free, and had over $3,000 left over to pay the family's bills. God moved in the hearts of people!

It was so much fun for me to watch my sons lead this project. It was even more fun to watch them watch God provide. It blew them away. They saw what I've seen many times before—how alive people feel when they're a tool in God's hands, making a difference with their lives. Nothing "same old" about that.

Making Ripples

I wonder how you get into a swimming pool. Any chance you might be a toe dipper? You stick your big toe in and you go, "Wooooo, that is cold!" And then your ankles, wooo, that's cold! Then your calves, wooo; your knees, wooo; your thighs, wooo! It's miserable!

You know what's really the best way to do it, don't you? Cannonball! You take a running start, tuck up your knees, hit the pool, and water goes flying everywhere! The ripples go out, hit the side, and come back in. They go back out and they come back in. They go back out and they come back in. If you're really big, that just keeps happening—and if the sides of that pool weren't there, they would just keep going and going, long after you made your initial splash.

I think that's what God had in mind for us. He's saying, "Trust me—jump! Make a splash with your one and only life, and we can make ripples together. Live your life in such a way that you touch someone else's life. Then they'll touch someone's life, and they'll touch someone's life—and long after you're dead and gone, the ripples will still be going strong."

I never dreamed I'd be a pastor, preacher, teacher

guy—never. And I certainly never dreamed I'd ever be that in Las Vegas. But one day I got a phone call from a guy out there named Gene Appel. He said, "Listen, our church is going to start a new church. Vegas is the fastest-growing city in the nation, and we want to locate this one on the fastest-growing side of the fastest-growing city because there's no church over there. We've just been praying, and we think you're the guy to do it."

I said, "Me?" I'm a Kentucky boy, and that just didn't seem like a logical fit. I thought to myself, "Doesn't 'Las Vegas church' sound like an oxymoron?" Then my imagination went into overdrive: Would there be "tithe machines" in the lobby—pull the lever and try to line up three burning bushes in a row? Might we

have bikini-clad women walking across the stage with placards to announce the hymn numbers? Would Wayne Newton be an elder?

I got my imagination under control and told Gene that Debbie and I would pray about it—although I really didn't plan on doing that. (I'm just being honest, here—c'mon, you might have said that, too!) But not only did we pray about it, we headed west to Vegas to check things out. And we felt like God was asking us to get out of our comfort zone—to take a chance, take a risk, to go there and plant a church in "Sin City."

By the way, we never called it Sin City. We called it the City of Grace, because the Bible says where sin abounds, grace abounds that much more (Romans 5:20). And we watched God's grace reach out to all kinds of broken, empty, stuck people and help them put their lives back together again. It was probably the greatest experience in my entire life. I learned more about the grace of God than I'd ever known, and I learned that no one is beyond God's love—no matter how far you might run, God runs farther. It was in Las Vegas that I finally began to grasp how high and long and wide and deep God's love for people really is. Ministering in Las Vegas was an awesome ride that has defined my ministry ever since.

I don't know if I rippled on a lot of people there, but I know for sure I rippled on a guy named Jeff. The two of us were playing in a pickup basketball game at the YMCA where our church met, when Jeff pulled me aside and said, "Man, I know we're here to play ball and all, but I wanted to let you know I've been coming to the church you've got going on here. It's pretty cool." I said, "Thanks, man, glad you like it."

He asked if we could talk for a few minutes, and as soon as we got started, he said, "I want to preface what I'm going to tell you by letting you know I'm a pretty smart guy. I have a degree in physics. I was a small college All-American quarterback. I own my own business, make a lot of money, and have a great family. I mean, I'm kind of one of those guys who's got it all together—except I don't really have it all together."

He admitted he'd had a gambling problem for a long time, that he drank too much, and that his life felt out of control—especially with the gambling. "I've been lying to my wife every night, telling her I'm working late," he said. "But man, I'm sitting in the casinos putting quarter after quarter, dollar after dollar in their video poker machines. I can't stop. The other night, I ran out to my car and started searching like a madman through the cushions to find some change so I could go back in and play some more. This is nuts! I feel like my life and my lies are all coming unraveled. Ever felt like that?" (I'm thinking, "Man, have I ever.")

Then he said, "I sit in church and get this feeling God might be able to help me. That maybe God's the answer."

I told him, "You're right. God can help you. He helped me."

Jeff and I began meeting, and to make a long story short, he ended up doing the same thing I did when I was seventeen. He humbled himself and asked Jesus Christ to be his leader. And God did a 180 with Jeff's life. He

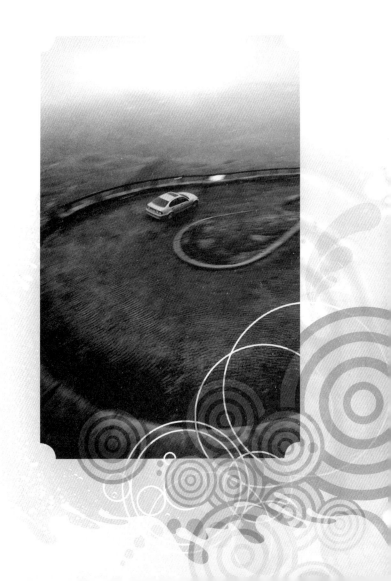

took away his desire to drink and gamble and gave him self-control to go along with his great personality and compassionate heart. Today, he's a dedicated husband and dad and one of the kindest, most dynamic, fired-up Christian guys I know.

Well, fast-forward a few months, and I get a phone call one night from this mom in St. Louis, Missouri. (I still don't know how she got my home number.) She said, "I have a twenty-one-year-old son named Gary who's got a drinking problem and a gambling problem. We think he's heading to Vegas, and we heard you have a church out there. Could you keep an eye out for him?"

I'm thinking, "Keep an eye out for him? Thirty million people come to Vegas every year. How am I supposed to find one kid?"

But finding one person in a crowd of thirty million is nothing for God. He is a relentless pursuer of our souls, and he tracked Gary down. About an hour later the mom called me back, saying, "He is in Vegas. Someone found him passed out in the parking lot of

Finding one person in a crowd of thirty million is nothing for God.

this little hotel, and the manager put him up for the night. Here's the address. Could you do something?"

I hung up wondering, "What am I gonna do?" But my next thought was, "Jeff! Yeah, I'll call Jeff!" As soon as he picked up the phone, I said, "Hey, I've got a

guy for you. He's at this little hotel down behind The Strip. Go get him!"

And Jeff said, "Okay, I'm on it."

At the time, we were a brand new church—a portable church that had to set up chairs and everything at 6 a.m. each Sunday. Jeff was part of that set-up crew. So at 5:30 a.m., he knocks on the door of this sleazy little hotel. A mountain of a guy swings open the door. At six-foot-four-inches tall and 250 pounds, Gary fills the doorframe. He's sleepy, hung over, got vomit on his shirt, and grunts out, "Yeah?"

Jeff is not deterred. "Hey, my name is Jeff, and I know all about you, man. Your mom called. You used to play football; I used to play football. You've got a drinking problem and a gambling problem; I used to have a drinking problem, I used to have a gambling problem. Come on, take a shower and let's go to church together."

Gary says, "Excuse me?"

But Jeff doesn't miss a beat. "Man, I'm sorry I'm talking so fast. And I'm sorry I'm here so early, but I'm on the set-up team at this new, really cool church and we set up at 6 a.m. And you're a big guy, so you could really help us. Come on, man—take a shower and let's talk about it in the car."

Gary stands there stunned and says, "Okay."

He took a shower, got in the car with a total stranger, and rode out to the high school where our church was meeting. He helped us set up chairs, then stayed for the service—and on that very day, like I did when I was seventeen and Jeff did when he was thirty-three—Gary surrendered his life to Jesus Christ. And God turned him completely around! By the time I left Las Vegas, Jeff was still rippling on Gary, and Gary had started rip-

**That's the way it goes!
One life touches a life, and
on and on the ripples go.**

pling on a guy named Chris, who had started rippling on a guy named Darnell. That's the way it goes! One life touches a life, who touches a life, who touches a life, and on and on the ripples go, long after you've made your splash.

When I think about Vegas, I also think of a girl I'll call Leah. When I first met her at the YMCA where we started our church, she was crying. By worldly standards, Leah was physically stunning. But I could see the emptiness and brokenness in her tear-filled eyes. Between sobs she told me, "I've never been a churchgoer. This is all new to me. I don't even know why I'm up here talking to you, or if this is even allowed. But my life sucks right now. I was going to have an abortion, but people talked me out of it. Now I've got this baby, and this baby doesn't like me!"

She went on to tell me she was a single mom who had never had a real example of how to be a good mother (her own mom had married five times). "I feel so lost and clueless. I don't know what to do. He's got colic and he cries all the time. What do I do with this baby?"

I said, "I don't have a clue either, but my wife Debbie is great with kids. Hang on a second."

I found Debbie, gave her a quick version of the story, and hooked her up with Leah. They sat down to talk, and by the time they'd finished, Debbie had invited Leah over for dinner. In fact, for the whole next year, Leah and her little boy came to our house for dinner every Sunday after church.

Now Leah's occupation was what they called a "wine goddess" at Caesar's Palace. She dressed in this really seductive Cleopatra-type outfit, and her looks and charm brought in enough tips to ensure a pretty good income. Debbie loved Leah. She mentored her and helped her be a good mom. It was pretty cool to watch her development—and fun to watch God slowly changing her. In fact, the more she grew to love God, the more veils she sewed on her costume.

One night she said, "Listen, my son is about to have his first birthday. I'm so grateful to God for blessing me with him, and I was thinking we might have a birthday party to celebrate. My apartment is a little small, though, and I want to invite some friends. Could we have the party at your house?"

"Sure, that'd be great," I said. She asked if I would take pictures, and I agreed to that, too.

Well, the night of party arrives, and at 7 p.m. the doorbell starts ringing. In walk all these other wine goddesses from Caesar's Palace! Leah's friends come into my living room, and I'm snapping pictures thinking, "God, when I said 'wherever,' I didn't think it would be in Vegas with a living room full of wine goddesses. This is unbelievable!"

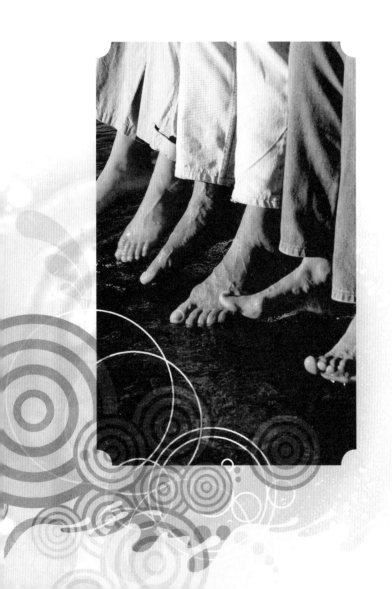

It's like that box of chocolates—you never know what you're going to get, you know?

Eventually, Leah gave her life to Christ. She put her life in the hands of the Destiny Maker. And now, years later, she's an awesome mom raising her two little boys to love God. She rippled on Lisa, who was there at the party that night, and Lisa is rippling on lots of other women these days. In fact, there was a whole contingent from Caesar's Palace who sat together in our church, soaking up the love and grace and wonder of God.

Right before I left Las Vegas, they told me, "We're working on the belly dancer at the club. She's going through a tough time, and we're trying to get her to come to church and stuff." And that's the way it happens. A life touches a life, who touches a life, who touches a life—and the ripples keep on going.

Ripples also make me think about Harold, one of my good friends in Kentucky—in fact, he's one of my favorite people on the planet. He's also the most country, good ole boy I know. There are a couple of things you'll never hear come out of Harold's mouth: "I'll take Shakespeare for $1,000, Alex," and "Checkmate." He's just this refreshingly uncultured, country-talkin', grateful-to-be-changed redneck!

When I first met him, he told me, "Mike, I know you've been out there in Sin City and all, and you've probably met lots of people who have done a lot of bad stuff. But I bet you never met anyone who's done some of the things I've done." And he was right. He began to pour out his sordid, destructive, dark past. He wasn't bragging. It wasn't that he was proud to be telling me these things; it was that he was broken. He was tired of floating around accidental-like. He needed God to fix him. He wanted to live.

Harold humbled himself before God and placed his life in the hands of the Destiny Maker and man, talk about making ripples. The guy is a cannonball machine! I can't begin to tell you how many people Harold's life has touched and is touching today. He's a walking example of what Jesus meant when he said that those who have been forgiven much, love much (Luke 7:47). He is one of the most grateful men I have ever met, and his gratitude touches people.

I interviewed Harold's small group one day in a church service—had them seated on stools in a straight line across the stage. Harold told a piece of his story, and then I asked him, "How did you get started on this new journey of yours?" He looked down the row of stools and pointed. "Stephen right there. He's the one that told me about this church and about this great God that could help me."

I said, "That's awesome," and turning to the guy seated next to Harold, I asked, "Luke, how did you get your life back on track?" He pointed and said, "Harold. Yeah, Harold and me are old fishing buddies. In fact, we used to do lines of cocaine together, but now we do lines of Scripture together—ain't that cool?"

"That's very cool," I said, and looked at the next guy with the question, "How did you get started on this new path?" He said, "Luke." And so it went all the way down

the line. One guy touched another guy's life, who touched another guy's life, who touched another guy's life! It's all about a life, touching a life, touching a life, touching a life.

It's impossible for me to talk to you about ripples without mentioning Nanny. She was our 103-year-old grandma before she passed away. Nanny was a trip! She was alive and funny and sharp up until the day she died.

I recently heard a 104-year-old woman respond to this question: "What's the best thing about being 104?" She replied, "No peer pressure!" I love that line, because it sounds just like something Nanny would have said. She once told me, "When you get to be 100, don't buy green bananas!" (Think about it.) And when Nanny turned 103, she said, "Now 103 is old." She'd pull back the sleeve of her little cotton housedress, just like the ones she wore every day of her life, and look at her watch. Then she'd say, "I bet my mom and sisters are standing around heaven wondering, 'Where in the world is Ida Mae? She should have been here by now. You don't think she went to that other place, do you?'" Nanny was something else.

When we had her 100th birthday party, I watched Nanny as she sat in her chair and greeted literally hundreds of people who'd come by her little cottage to say thank you to this simple, tiny, beautifully wrinkled woman. Nanny never learned to drive, never went to college, never had any money to speak of, and never had her name in the paper (except on the day she turned 100). She lived the last forty years of her life as a widow in the same little-bitty house where she raised six girls (with one bathroom!).

That was pretty much her claim to fame.

But you see, she decided early on that she was going to put herself in the hands of the Destiny Maker and simply pour her life and her love and her faith into those six girls. And you know what those six girls did? They poured their lives and their love and their faith into their three or four kids. And their kids poured their lives and their love and their faith into their three or four kids. And now all these people, many of whom had never even met Nanny, came through that house to say, "Thank you for the way you've touched my life."

The cool part of the story for me is that one of those kids Nanny raised was a girl named Molly. Who had this incredibly cute daughter named Debbie, who changed my life. See how it goes?

Rippling Forward

Debbie and I have a daughter named Jodi who now has two little girls of her own. It's neat to watch her interact with them and to know what a difference she's going to make in their lives, just like Nanny did in the lives of her kids. It's especially gratifying when we think back to Jodi's junior year of high school.

That was when she kind of lost track of God—or maybe she was just trying to find him in a lot of different ways. She was a float-around kind of girl for a while, and there were some pretty destructive things going on. Let me say to every parent who may be reading this that you can do the best job possible of being a parent, but your kids are still individuals with free will. They make their own choices. You lavish them with unconditional love and set good, loving boundaries for them. But they can still lie to you and do things you never dreamed they would do. That's reality.

And during that year, we often had to pray, "God, she's your kid. We will do the best job we can at being her parents, but we can't be with her all the time. We can't, but you can." We prayed two things: that Jodi would possess godly discernment and that she would be a lousy liar. And she was.

Her life (like that of another seventeen-year-old I knew) began to unravel. She couldn't remember

We prayed two things: that Jodi would possess godly discernment and that she would be a lousy liar. And she was.

which lie she told to whom or who knew what she did and where she was when she did it. She was exhausted trying to live two lives. She humbled herself and raised her hands up in the air and surrendered her life to the forgiveness and loving leadership of the Destiny Maker. And she is an amazing young woman these days.

When she graduated from high school, Jodi said, "Listen, I want to make my life count. I don't think I want to go to school right away." A few years earlier, our family had gone on a short-term mission trip to Haiti. Jodi informed us, "I'd like to go back to Haiti and work for a year with those orphans and the poor people at the medical mission."

I said, "Jo, you do know that Haiti's the poorest country in the Western Hemisphere? It's AIDS infested and it's voodoo controlled. You wanna live there?"

She said, "I fell in love with those kids, and I think God wants me to give a year of my life to do that."

I said, "Alright. If you feel God is stirring in you to do that, we're excited for you."

Well, "excited" wasn't a real authentic thing to say,

because one of the hardest things I ever did was to put that girl on a plane and say, "See ya later, Jodi." I went out in the parking lot of the airport and cried like the artsy guy I am. I prayed like I had two years earlier, "God, she's your kid."

She was in a pretty remote area of the island where communication was a bit complicated. That year, Debbie's and my three favorite words were, "You've got mail!" Because email was the only way we could communicate with Jodi.

One night, we got an email from her that went something like this:

Mom, Dad, this was the most phe-
nomenal night of my life. Someone came
and got me in the middle of the night to

help deliver a baby! I got to this little hut and there's this naked, screaming, pregnant woman lying on the dirt floor. They called me because they saw me with the nurse and thought I was a nurse. But I don't know how to deliver babies; I just kind of assisted once. And I'm there in this hut by myself, thinking, "I'm eighteen years old, in a third-world country, in the middle of a jungle, by myself, with a flashlight and a screaming, naked, pregnant woman lying on the dirt floor of a hut and I'm gonna have to deliver this baby. What am I doing here?"

To make matters worse, a visitor walked in the hut. She was dressed in the blue and red

wardrobe of a voodoo witch doctor. She be-
gan to chant some evil incantation thing. She
walked around me and the pregnant woman,
stopping at the woman's stomach to put some
kind of oil on it. Then she reversed her walk
around us, all the while chanting something in
Creole. She stopped at the woman's head and
put the same kind of oil on her head and then
stood there chanting and staring at me with
the most evil glare I've ever seen.

I'm getting ready to deliver this baby and
I'm thinking, "I'm eighteen years old; I'm in
a third-world country, three thousand miles
away from home; I'm in a hut with a naked,
screaming, pregnant woman lying on the floor;

I've got a flashlight and a voodoo woman staring an evil hole through me!"

I didn't know what to do. I just looked right back at her, and I knew she didn't understand English, but I started singing: "Our God is an awesome God; He reigns from heaven above; with wisdom, power and love, our God is an awesome God." Then the voodoo woman grabbed all of her stuff and ran out of the hut.

I knew then that this little baby was going to be born with the blessing of God and not the curse of Satan.

I'm reading this email as Jodi's dad, thinking, "What are you doing in a hut with a voodoo woman? You get on a plane tomorrow and you get back here! We've got pizza and ice cream and puppies and fluffy pillows—come on home!"

But in the next breath I said right out loud, "Way to go, Jodi. Way to ripple, girl."

You see, who knows who that little baby's going to grow up to be and whose lives he or she is going to touch, and whose lives they're going to touch, and whose lives they're going to touch. All because one courageous eighteen-year-old girl said, "I'm tired of floating around accidental-like, like a feather on a breeze. I want to put my life in the hands of the Destiny Maker. I want to make some ripples with my life."

Jesus said, "Only those who throw away their lives for my sake and for the sake of the Good News will ever know what it means to really live" (Mark 8:35 LB).

"I'm tired of floating around accidental-like, like a feather on a breeze. I want to put my life in the hands of the Destiny Maker. I want to make some ripples with my life."

Do you want to really live? I think you have a choice right now. You can close this book, throw it on a shelf or in a trashcan, and choose to float around accidental-like, like a feather on the breeze—all your life, if you want to. Or you can put yourself in the loving

hands of the Destiny Maker and watch him fill your life with purpose and direction and passion and meaning. Hear him say, "I made you, I love you, and my plans for you are to give you a hope and a future you could only imagine. Come on, let me lead your life. We'll make some ripples together!"

And that's all I have to say about that.

PHOTO CREDITS AND COPYRIGHT

Breaux family photo archives: 97, 107

Corbis: 80

Dreamstime: 13, 93

Getty Images: 8, 16, 21, 30, 33, 36, 52, 57, 58, 68, 72, 77, 87, 88, 98

Jupiter Images: 24, 63, 110

Masterfile: 26, 40–41, 44

. . . .

All photos used with permission.

. . . .

WILLOW

Willow Creek Association
P.O. Box 3188
Barrington, Illinois 60010-3188
www.willowcreek.com